Hope I Make It Before Y'all Take It

Alcee H. Walker

PublishAmerica
Baltimore

© 2009 by Alcee H. Walker.
All rights reserved. No part of this book may be reproduced, stored in a retrieval system or transmitted in any form or by any means without the prior written permission of the publishers, except by a reviewer who may quote brief passages in a review to be printed in a newspaper, magazine or journal.

First printing

PublishAmerica has allowed this work to remain exactly as the author intended, verbatim, without editorial input.

ISBN: 978-1-60749-349-5
PUBLISHED BY PUBLISHAMERICA, LLLP
www.publishamerica.com
Baltimore

Printed in the United States of America

"I told my momma I was gon be the one but she ain't believe me"

-Torrance Hatch

Introduction

"If an American, because his skin is dark, cannot eat in a restaurant, cannot send his children to the best public school available, cannot vote for the elected officials who represent him, then who among us would be content to have the color of his skin changed and stand in his place?"—President John F Kennedy

The concept of living in Florida encapsulates an enormity of wealth, the beach, and the idea of sunshine that serves as hope from the endless Northeastern winters. There are times however, when the Florida sunshine escapes its underprivileged neighborhoods.

My story is one such account. When I was born, I was very different from the rest of my family. I was a premature baby with a birth weight of 2 pounds 6 ounces. I guess this is considered lucky because there was thought from my parents about having an abortion. My grandmother on my mother's side did not want an abortion while my grandmother on my father's side did want my mother to have an abortion. However, my father did not have the money to get an abortion, thankfully for me. I had no idea about any of this until I was twenty years old. It was not such a great feeling hearing them throw that word "abortion" around so freely with me right there. [Expectedly, I was hospitalized for some time until I was healthy enough to leave the hospital.]

As a baby, I was really close to my grandmother who always called me an angel baby. Now that I am much older, I feel like she called me this because my parents were thinking about having an abortion. Then, after being premature, there was another risk that maybe I was not going to stay on this earth, but I made it. I am here. She was thankful for that and I think her faith in me set me up for a successful life no matter what came my way.

My grandmother always said that I was her favorite grandchild and that she would always be there for me, but she later passed away. If she was still here, I know my life would be very different and I would not have experience, as many of the negative aspects of my childhood because I know my grandmother would have protected me. After I had interviewed members of my family this past year, I learned even more about my wonderful grandmother. I was informed that my grandmother was absolutely crazy about me. When I was little, I would watch the movie "Home Alone" over and over and over again. I would not let anyone in my family change the movie; I would guard the television and prevent anyone from touching my favorite movie. The only person who didn't get angry with me and was so patient and kind, was my grandmother. She would sit there with me and watch it every single time.

She was so patient with me in terms of everything. I had an extremely hard time as a little boy distinguishing an apple from a tomato. I would go into the fridge and bite into one as if it were an apple. My grandmother would stand in front of me and laugh about it while everyone else grew impatient of my mistake.

I was four years old when my grandmother passed away. I can just barely remember sitting in the front row of the funeral looking around at the crying faces. I had no idea why everyone was so upset, of why my grandmother was laying in the casket, and why that was the beginning of my life being passed on from family member to family member. My family members knew I made a big impact on my grandmother's life and she prayed for me to make it with such a bad situation at hand. I can still hear the lady at the church singing and the state everyone was in over the death of my grandmother.

After my grandmother passed away, my mom and I were living with my Aunt Tammy James who had two kids at the time. My mother was still so young, so she was still out on the streets getting into trouble. Aunt Tammy was really my cousin but because she was so good to me, I called her my aunt my whole life.

At age seven and in 1st grade, since I never got much attention at home, I was always excited to go school and be with my classmates. I loved running around at recess and I felt like I had so much more freedom when I was at school. I had transferred Elementary schools so I was the "new kid" and really wanted to fit in. In Physical Education, we were having a race to see who was the fastest kid in the class. [I knew I was always fast but did not know any of these kids.] I won an award in the class for being the fastest kid. I was really excited and just couldn't wait to take it home and show my friends and family.

I was walking home with the award in my hand. I did not want to put it in my book bag. I was so thrilled with myself and couldn't wait to see how proud my family would be. When I got home, I showed it to my oldest sister who was really proud of me and wanted to hang the award on the wall for me. She rushed to the room with the award to nail it up for me. She asked me to look for a hammer. We didn't have a hammer so she told me not to worry about it. So she got a deodorant spray bottle and wanted to use the bottle as a hammer. Neither of us knew if it would work or not, it just seemed like a good idea at the time. She jumped onto the bed and then jumped on top of the dresser. She started to bang the bottle to the nail and right before my eyes there was a big fire that lasted about 5 seconds. It came at me so fast, before I could turn away or anything. I just panicked. I was screaming for my mother but once again, she was nowhere to be found.

This fire burned my face, legs, and arms over nearly my entire body. My little cousin was in the room and her burns were just as bad as mine. [I thought I was going to die the pain was so severe.] We rushed out of the room and ran outside while everyone in the house was screaming "Call 911!" My aunt sprayed us down with a water hose, which really did hurt and made the situation even worse in the end. The ambulance came and I was so afraid of getting in the vehicle because I thought that I was going to die. I used to think that only people who were going to die had to get into an ambulance. I was just screaming and crying for my mother. "I don't want to get in there, I don't want to get in there!" I cried out over and over.

When I finally got in and reached the hospital my cousin and I were put under these machines for about 24 hours. I had no idea on what was going on and just was repeatedly saying to myself I don't want to die. We had IVs and oxygen masks attached to us. We had no idea what was going to happen at that point, we were just so scared. We were wrapped in special towels that would help our skin stop bleeding and hold our peeling skin together. I can remember lying in the bed with all this wrapping and machinery on me. I turned over and could see my father, my aunts, and my cousins all looking through the window just crying at the sight of me.

Two months later we were allowed to go home but still had to attend rehab. We had to get up every morning and get into a boiling hot tub of water. The tub was huge. We had to climb up a ladder and sit in the tub for about thirty minutes every day. The hot water would peel all the dead skin off of our bodies. It was so painful; I just wanted it to be over.

I went from loving school to almost refusing to go. My face was still marked up because of the burns. I always had to wear long pants because of the scars on my legs. When I returned to school, I was ashamed of going to class because I would get picked on and was called "burnt face," "burnt boy," and "burnt legs." There was this one girl who I really liked. Her name was Samantha and I thought she would not like me after looking like this. I just wanted to wait until everything was cleared up so that I looked better but I had to go to school; I had already missed so much.

I grew up in Riviera Beach, Florida. As I got older, growing up in a low-income family and living in a low-class environment where people are getting killed daily had a big influence on my life. When I saw crimes like stealing and then running from the police, which the older kids did on my block. I thought it was cool and I would do the same. Since I did not have any guidance from my family, I thought stealing from the store and getting in trouble with my friends would be cool. I wanted to fit in with the older guys and be popular and I thought this was the way.

I have been in the back seat of the police car several times because of crimes I decided to commit with my friends. We used to steal these toy motor race cars 5out of K-mart. One time these undercover cops stopped us from leaving. I was with my older sister Barbara, who I was crying for when they were taking us to the back of the store. They put handcuffs on us and put us into the back of the car until my parents came to take us home.

Another time, it was around Christmas time, and everyone wanted a motor scooter. Neither my friends nor I got one for Christmas. So, we decided to take a bus to go into what we called the "cracker town." In this town, you have all the upper class people. As we were going through the neighborhood, we came across one of those motor scooters. I saw it first and since we all wanted it, I had to go after it. There was no one in the yard outside and the scooter was just sitting there. I decided to creep up slowly in the yard and grab it. I didn't want to start the motor, so I just took it and ran. My friends had already taken off running. Before I knew it, there was a guy running out of the house screaming, "what are you doing?!" At that moment, my heart just dropped. I just needed to get away. The man hopped in his truck and my friends were gone. I was the only one there and I really wanted to have the scooter and was determined to have it. I finally just stopped to crank the motor and go. But when I did that, the guy was right behind me with the truck. There was a lady driving the truck and two men in the back. The guys reached out of their window and grabbed my shirt and pulled over to the side. They were screaming to call the police. I was terrified. I did not know what to do at this point. They were asking me all sorts of questions waiting for the police to come. They asked me where I was from, where my parents were, how old I was. The man was holding me so tight. After about ten minutes, the police came. The officer got out of his vehicle and put me into handcuffs after the man explained the situation. Right before he put me into the police car, I saw my friends walking down the street and they did not even come over to see me. He put me in the back of his car and I had to give him all my information. He also wanted the information of the people I was with. I gave him fake names because I did not believe in telling on my friends. I just sat in the back for about an hour. He then lectured me on how I can't do those things anymore because I will end up in jail someday and then let me go. Since I was young, the family did not press charges on me. I was then on my way.

I am a sophomore football player at St. Lawrence University. I am from West Palm Beach, FL– a success story but it wasn't always like this for myself. This is a story of struggle, a story of failures, a story of the projects, a story of theft, a story of alienation, and a story of tears but most importantly this is a story of triumph. With dark gloomy days that [pranced my life] in sunny Florida, this is an illuminating story that reveals the truth about America, a country where opportunity and hope go hand in hand. There are also people who have negatively affected my life and unfortunately my parents are two of them, which hurts for anyone to have to say about their parents.

I ask myself, is every kid from the hood like myself? Why can't other African American children see the light at the end of the tunnel? What is it about these neighborhoods that even America refuses to acknowledge? How can we instill education, hope, and opportunity into these neighborhoods instead of violence, drug abuse, and hunger?

My life story acts as a unique lens, one that humanizes these problems and offers so many opportunities where someone could have stepped up and made the difference. Such opportunities need to be capitalized. I have changed my life already, a kid from the hood who has already done more than what ordinary people from my background cannot accomplish in a lifetime. My story is where we can find hope; it is a tale that highlights the possibilities and opportunities to make a difference, and a narrative that will make you question the society we live in.

The purpose behind sharing my story is not to glorify one individual, who despite the odds, made it. I am an individual who overcame the odds and went above and beyond in demonstrating my level of commitment to a future—a future where perhaps some of my pain may be subdued. Today, we live in an America that continues to ignore the struggles of underpreviledged black neighbors unless there is a riot or a drive-by epidemic. College students can take advantage of every political and social platform the US has to offer but typically they are the first to take a big step back when it comes to volunteer work. While the circumstances today are different from that of the civil rights movement, there is an observable lack of engagement and concern for the future of these neighborhoods and what they hold that is so exclusive. Considering America's current involvment abroad coupled with rising levels of domestic hunger, homlessness, and racial struggles, the country's youth and silent majority remains comparatively uninvolved. There is no visible "Vietnam Syndrome" where students and young adults take to the streets. President John F Kennedy always said that "the cost of freedom is always high – but Americans have always paid it." Today it is paid with a credit card.

Chapter 1: Andre Calvin White, My Biological Father

"You see, at one point I didn't think you was my son. Your momma and your grand momma wanted to have an abortion. I didn't have the money to pay for an abortion."
-Andre White speaking on his son Alcee Walker

    It is indisputably a fact that parents play a key role in one's life. From before one is born, to the first time he cries when brought into this world, from the first time he walks, to the first time he falls, from the first time he wins an award, to the first time he fails a class – if anyone, one's parents are the two definite individuals who bear the promise of unconditional love and support. This is the way we know nature works.

    My parents did not play the usual role of caring, nurturing, supportive people in my life. My father, Andre White, was 24 years old when he impregnated my mother, Caurise Walker, who was only 16 at the time. "When I first met her, she lied about her age – she told me that she was eighteen. I was shocked when I first found out that she was pregnant and only sixteen! If something like that happens now, where a twenty-four year old man makes a sixteen year old girl pregnant – I would go to jail!" said my father reflecting on his vague and disappearing memories of my mother.

    I never had a real relationship with my father. My father rarely made an effort to interact with me. When I did speak with him, he would always tell lies. I first spoke to my father when I was in the third grade when he picked me up to go purchase me some tennis shoes for school. I didn't know what to say to him and I was a little afraid because I didn't know him. Even though he was my father, I didn't feel comfortable around him.

My father first saw me when I was born; he claims to have had problems with my mother Caurise. "At the time I had somebody else – another woman and that's one part of it and there were a lot of other little things. Because of my problems with your mother and your family, I saw you less during your younger days but when you grew older I saw you more – your younger days, I wasn't so much around," said my now forty-four year old father.

This past year, I went home for my spring break. After all these years, I was determined to meet with my father and ask him some of the questions that have been on my mind my whole life.

I interviewed my father on a bright sunny afternoon in West Palm Beach, Florida. I arrived at his current girlfriend's house prior to the time I scheduled to interview him. It has been two years since I seen or spoken to him. The last time I saw him was at the gas station for a quick second. He told me that he had a few bucks for me before I went off to college. Just like he had been absent from my life, I never saw those few bucks. Before I interviewed him, our relationship lacked not only in communication but trust as well. Every time we saw each other in public our conversation would only last for a few seconds. It was twenty minutes later when he arrived in a car with a woman wearing a torn grey worker unisuit. He asked me to wait as he quickly ran into the house. My father was 6'4, about two hundred pounds and had a few dreadlocks on his head. His mouth was filled with a few gold teeth and he had a limp in his walk as if he was a pimp. Upon his return, we drove around the block to the park in my car. When we reached the park I could feel a cluster of butterflies in my stomach and my heart was beating really fast. I had that same nervous feeling like when they were calling my name at my high school graduation. When finally made it to the park and we decided to sit on the benches facing the park where three little kids were playing on the swings. There was a dog barking as if he had lost his owner and a fisherman fishing in the nearby lake.

As a child, it was tough for me to think of him because I was confused as to what his real feelings might have been, [perhaps even scared.] All of my sisters' fathers have been in their lives and I was the only sibling without a father in my life. At Christmas, they would get all of the gifts and I would be resentful and always wished I had a father that did the same for me. Every time I would call the phone number he gave me I would either get a voicemail or no answer. These memories are what I am left with for my cold walks back from the football field during the arctic fury of the North Country.

My Father was an alcoholic. He spent most of his money on beer and other alcoholic beverages. As I got older, I tried to refrain from the distant yet, direct and painful memories of my father absence. After a while, I started to ignore the situation and moved on with my life, but did I? As the baby on my father's side of the family, I never had a chance to build a relationship with my two oldest brothers and my oldest sister whom I've never met.

During my conversation with him, I stumbled upon an array of questions. I asked him his age and when I was born. He replied, "Let's see, I'm forty-four now and you [looking at me] are twenty one?"

"I'm twenty," I responded.

"Ok so I was twenty four years old but your momma was something like sixteen! I first met her at this place where we all used to hang out – we went to a concert together at the place that stood where the mall is now," he remembered. "We became friends and one thing led to another I guess."

I asked him when he had last seen my mother?

"Last time I saw her? Well, last time I saw her – to be honest with you – it might have been …. I don't know… the time when she moved from her previous place or it might have been the time that she was going to move. It might have been November of last year," he replied in a confused way trying to refresh his memory. "I don't really see her much. The last time I saw her was when I fixed her television for her back in November."

Where everyday struggles of a teenager in school can be overwhelming, living in the hood can be even more troublesome. Moving from place to place and from one relative to another, I never learned to call one place home. I asked my father what were his thoughts of a child, any child, being left on his own without a father or a father figure?

He shrugged his shoulders and said: "I know – I know. But I had other kids and they are the same way. Like I said, I was young and I just…Bottom line is that I did not want to settle down. I could not be with this woman and I was just hanging in the streets, hustling, trying to have ends meet.

Attempting to get my father to answer my question, "how would this relate to my life?," I pushed him to be more honest.

"I personally may have wanted to be with your mom but your grandmomma – we didn't see eye to eye. It was a lot of things that went down. Like I said right, I'm sorry .... I'm sorry I didn't raise you like that but I was really .... How do they say it .... Not ready to have a kid."

My father struggled to raise me "like that" and what the term "like that" really means – I still have utterly no idea. Is it my fault that I was brought into this world? Why do men and women from underprivileged neighborhoods continue to have children when their own basic individual needs are in jeopardy?

(Carrying an ocean full of thoughts and questions,) I was starting to feel dizzy at this point and my head felt fuzzy.

"Do you think that bringing someone into this world brings a sense of responsibility?" I asked him this question attempting to steer the conversation back to the main goal of this interview, to see what went wrong.

"True, True. See, I, at one point, didn't think you were my son. Your momma and your grand momma wanted to have an abortion. I didn't have the money to pay for an abortion. You were born and born prematurely as your mother had the baby ... she had the baby," remarked a confused, slow, and tired father who was trying to gather his own thoughts' "I was saying that the baby was not mine, which you didn't look like me. So we had the blood test, turned out to be my little boy – I was shocked. So what had happened was, the blood test came out and they were saying that you was 99.3% mine! From then on, now I'm on a different route."

"How long after my birth did you have the blood test done?" I asked him, trying to make sense of the whole situation.

"You were born what...1988?" he said.

"1989!" I roared.

A shell-shocked Andre quickly replied: "No man! For real?"

I could not muster the energy to say anything back to a father who couldn't remember the year his own son was born.

My father had the blood test done two years after my birth when my mother decided to claim child support. Andre was broke and in denial. I was not the gift from God he asked for.

Here's the only insight my father could offer on the subject: "Like I said, once I found out you were my son I tried to be there. I had problems with your momma but between now and back then, it's a whole different world between us." I still can't tell whom he referred to as he used the words "better us." Perhaps you have grown a few inches in height from back then and hybrid cars roam our streets today, but his world of relationships and family are still the same – it is torn.

The wind started to pick up at this point and our interview release papers blew away. [As I galloped to save the pages and progressed asking Andre if he ever made the effort visit me.]

Followed by another pause and a glance into the wind he replied, "I heard you were with your uncle or something. Truth is though, I had other women – I mean I feel bad – I feel real bad that I wasn't with you coming up but … I had to go through child support! You know what I'm saying? I'd rather directly give you the money." A broken relationship and a shattered world was all my father could ever realistically offer.

"If you had the opportunity to make everything right and be there for me, would you have done differently?" Silence followed. I rephrased: "So say you're 24 again, I am just a little boy – everything is different and you were with my mom or whoever – What would you have done differently?"

"To be honest with you, right now…" he tried to finish his sentence but was interrupted by a call on his cell phone. "Sorry, yea … if I could have started out all over, I would have seen if I could've grabbed you…To stay with me! Now, I have …. Like… Visitation rights. Back then, I had no visitation rights." I pondered visitation rights, visitation rights to see your own son?

Feeling that my question was still unanswered I asked again, "But what exactly would you have done differently, what would you have done for me?"

He coughed and replied, "I didn't provide for you because I had child support."

I was getting frustrated here. Biting all shame, I asked again, "what exactly and precisely would you have done differently for me?"

"If you were living with me?" he inquired as if I had asked him a question from the SATs.

"Yes sir," I said smiling.

"I don't think you would have been different than you are now!" he took a short pause, spitted in the grass and continued "Because I don't feel any hurting for nothing – you would have been as smart as you are now."

"Often times it is not about the smarts, it is about the opportunity," I said with a combined mix of some frustration but mostly disappointment.

"The opportunity to like … doing more things for you?" He replied in a clueless manner.

"The opportunity for me to have a place, the opportunity to have access to books, the opportunity to be relieved from where I was going to get the next dollar to pay for my gas or bills when I was living on my own." I responded to him with a slightly loud voice, I was getting frustrated thinking that my questions were not that difficult.

"Well, your momma had other children so she put you as a last child." My father scratched his head. "You had a sister older than you and such but if you had stayed with me?"

"Yes!" I replied with a smile that could have been mistaken for a smirk.

"None of my children stayed with me," he said. "I had two that stayed with me but after they turned five or six, they went with their mothers. Only thing I could have provided for them was shelter, clothes, tried to be a father. I'm not rich, if you were staying with me, you would have probably had to move from place to place."

Trying to gauge his financial situation I ask, "What are some of the jobs you've had thus far?"

After being spaced out for a few moments, looking up into the sky wondering when these questions are going to end he replied, "I'm a small engine generator. I fix chainsaws. I've been working on it for the last eighteen years."

"But you said you were a hustler earlier?" I inquire to try and connect the dots.

"Right, that hustling life it was tough," says my father with a slight smile on his face. "I wish I didn't have to worry about where my next dollar was going to come from."

"Did you ever get in trouble with the law?" I was embarrassed asking this of him.

"Yea, yea. I've been in the law, but I've never been in trouble with the law for when I was hustling. I have got in trouble for unnecessary things."

"Like?" Now I am curious.

"Let me see. I have been accused of burglary, I have been accused of trespassing on unwanted property, and I have been accused of running from the law—like driving. But I have only one restriction on me for driving. All the others I was accused of, I have gotten off." he remarked. "Every person has right to a trial until proven guilty – I was not proven guilty." I could sense that his voice lacked the confidence of truth.

"Now that I am in college and doing well for myself, do you think there is a time or a place where you could fix anything?" I ask this thinking that perhaps Andre never got the opportunity to share his love.

Things that I would have changed?" he asks.

"Yes and things that you still could," I say.

"I would have spent more time with you when you were coming up." My father replied with a feeble voice. "Before you went to college, I would have had you be with me, to hang with me."

Not impressed I asked: "But life is still going, you are forty four and I am 20 – what can happen now or in the future that would be different?

"Can you imagine how many football games I've played dad?" I said with a smile.

"You know, I'm going to tell you," said my father completely brushing off what I had just asked him. "At the time you were playing football, it was during your younger days. I never saw you at a college game. You can ask your two other brothers; they also compete. You can ask them, I never had a chance to see them play. I would love to see you play though, you know?"

Appalled by watching my father ignore the question I asked him: "How do you think that makes me feel? How would not having parents at their child's games make any kid feel?"

"Like if their daddy wasn't there to see them on the field?" Yes, I say with an annoyed look on my face.

"That was one of my faults and I wish I could change that," said my father whispering the words 'second chance' under his breath. "I have so much time in my heart that has gone by, and I wish I could be there."

"Have you considered coming down for any of my college games?" I asked.

"I have one problem, I know it's not a big thing but I'm scared of flying," for just a few seconds, he looked embarrassed, even vulnerable.

"You could drive?" I said wondering.

"Yea that's no excuse, I know," he responded in a high pitch voice. "I know that and I would love to but the last time I left the state of Florida was nineteen years ago. So it will be kind of like big for me but …."

"Do you not think that I deserved that as your kid?" I tried to fill in as he attempted to zone out again, with his head facing toward the ground and his eyes closed.

"You're right …. I could – I could – I could." He replied followed by a silence.

"Anything else you would like to say?" I was running out of questions. "Truth is, I am bitter about my life and my relationship with you."

"And I would be too, I would be too but I'm not the whole fault – I would be too, but I am not the whole fault." he said to himself. "Your momma and I didn't get along. I understand things though, this is not the first time I've heard it. But there is nothing I could do … all along."

"As a college student I can tell you that there are times when I need things up at school," I tried to give my father some context. "Times when I run out of supplies and money on my meal plan. Do you think there are things that you could/could've facilitated for me?"

"One thing I know about my son, you're not going to give up," he stops to cough. "If you want something and you cannot have it, you will leave it alone, you would not have it."

Saddened by his answer I replied, "But isn't a part of being a child or growing up dreaming—a chance to seeing what you can have rather than leaving it alone?"

After a long pause he replies, "I am right now in the predicament where I don't have a driving license. I owe $48,000 in child support – I owe your mom $32,000 – and I owe your two brothers the balance of the two. Calculation isn't right. It is very rough for me right now, once I get through it – I mean I work for paycheck to paycheck. If I have anything else left and you called me, it might not be exactly what you ask for but I could give you some. But I have to know in advance … and …"

"Anything that you would like to say to me at this point, anything you have never said to me before, something that you couldn't say to me before perhaps?"

"Only thing I could tell you son," he looked at me for the first time. "I love you – I love you. I wish I could do it again, wish I could start over with life. A lot of things right now, a lot of things … I'm not rock bottom – I'm living but it's hard."

Unsatisfied I ask again, "Anything that you haven't said to me before that you would like to say?"

"I love you man… I love you," he says.

Feeling disgusted, I fired back: "You've never said that to me before"

"No man, no – I have. That doesn't sound right." My fathered paused, took a deep breath and shook his head from left to right for a while. "Something I have never said before? Only thing I can tell you – keep your head up and be strong and you already knows that."

"It was devastating to know that my biological dad wanted to have an abortion, but what stood in the way was not enough funds. I look forward to seeing what type of changes we could make to build a relationship" – Alcee Walker speaking his father, Andre White.

Chapter 2: My Sixteen Year Old Birth Mother, Caurise Lynndell Walker

"Some mommas murder their kids but I just hit you with a glass plate, I can't take that back, its over with and all we can do is move on!"
-Caurise Walker, speaking on her son, Alcee Walker

When I decided to write this book, I needed to dig deeper for information regarding my mom. She was not absent like my father. I wanted to know why she didn't treat me right, why she hit me with a plate, why my brothers and sisters didn't live with me, why she was in jail on Christmas, why we don't see eye to eye. I tried to get answers to these questions over spring break by interviewing her. My mother and I never really had a great relationship. As I walked to her front door, I remembered all the times she cursed at me and all the times I was mistreated. She lived in a tangerine orange and white condo apartment. It had three bedrooms, two baths and a nice yard. It was a very quiet neighborhood and no one was in sight. I knew she wouldn't want to do the interview because of some of the questions I was going to ask her. I didn't want her to curse at me like she use to and the day before I had already told her what I was coming to do. I told her that I was really serious about interviewing her. When she opened the door I greeted her right away with a good morning and she greeted back with a mean look as if she was sick to her stomach "Hey."

As I entered the apartment, I noticed that there were dishes all over the kitchen like they were sitting for a couple of days. This reminded of when I was younger and I had to clean up after school everyday. I walked into the living room that was furnished with large couches with comfy pillows, a 50-inch flat screen TV and there was a painting on the wall of man on a horse that I remembered from my childhood. I waited for her in the living room while she yelled to my little brother Juan to come downstairs to wash the dishes. I had a flashback of a time when I was yelled at to come wash the dishes. Once I was settled I began telling my mother that the purpose of interviewing her was not to point fingers or tell the world how badly she treated me, but I was hurt and I felt like we still had animosity toward one another. I just wanted to know why I was treated the way I was treated and what I did for her to do the things she did to me.

I slowly sat down with my heart beating fast as if I just finished a marathon. I got right to it asking my mother, What does family mean to you?

"Togetherness," she said mustering an innocent face, but with a look as if ask why I am questioning her.

So," I shrugged, "what do you think of me?"

"I think you're a little conceited sometimes, probably don't mean to. Other than that you're a good kid," said the mother who had never made the effort to know her child.

"And how old were you when you had me?" I asked her.

With a calm and relaxed look, she said, "When I had you I was about 15. But I had your sister previously at the age of 13."

Marveled at her boldness and confidence I continued to question, "You mentioned the word togetherness but most of us didn't live with you."

"Yea that's true," she responded back in an aggressive voice, defending herself. This voice reminded me of when she used to yell at me for not taking out the trash. "But you know it was the choices that I made, when I was having my kids, I was a minor so my mom had to place my kids."

"She made the choice as to where a child of mine was going to go." "It's not really... Like I didn't want to keep them together – it was more like she placed them where she wanted to – decisions were already made, I had nothing to do." You were the same. She had spoken to everybody and I couldn't touch it. I always help support them. Even though I didn't know where they were I always tried to support them."

Wanting to know more about my grandmother, I asked her, "What was my grandmother like?"

"She... she... I could say she was a single mom. She was very strict; she was a single mom. By that I mean we got whoopings when we did something wrong. Whatever she said, went." My mother said as a response to my question like it didn't mean anything.

How were you raised? What was the environment like?

"Umm ... rough... rough neighborhood ... in the hood. We were all raised in poverty places."

I didn't like living with you, but if I needed a place to stay over break, could I stay with you?

"YEA ... you could, you could drive my car and do everything ... yea you could. I don't know why you don't want to"

How about my brothers and sisters?

"Yea ... of course ... your sister comes by the house. They welcome anytime. But see my yall don't play by my rules. I'm not the kind of mom who does everything – when you were in school you kind of did whatever you wanted with your money. I took care of the bills and everything, I didn't ask for a dime. I don't believe in that – I believe – Like my daughter Caryan she doesn't want to do anything – she doesn't want to go to school, she doesn't abide by the rules. When she's here and I come back, she's having a party

… you know…. And I'm just not that type of mom and she won't abide by my rules. She's 18 and I teach all my kids, as I got older, I gave it a try. Ashley pretty much thinks that my house is old, it's boring and it's too far. It's just an excuse for all of them and then they turn around on me, just like you. What mother would tell a child "Oh you can't come and be here? No one would say that. I don't care where I am at and what I'm doing, my children are always welcome. I'm not gonna run down the street. Whenever they want to come they're welcome. I don't even want to be here, I'll leave the keys and the remote controls. That's pretty much how that goes."

As I continued to interview her, I heard Juan in the background washing dishes and Jayvon asking Juan to fix him some breakfast.

You said that you believed in providing for your children, is that something you were able to do for me?

"Uhhhhhhhh … when you went to college, before that yea… you know I was working two jobs and I was able to put it up. But with the economy and all, it's been shaky. But if you call me, I know you need me and I would but for the most part you are the one who's led yourself out. When you need me I'd pick up the phone and be like hey I need this I need that just like the other kids and I would take care of them. That's how that pretty much works."

Tell me about my father.

"Loser! Big time," she giggled like I made a funny statement. "I dated him … that was years ago. I was a young girl, just 15 and he was an adult so I never connected that…. You know we…. We never … we dated like maybe a year and that was it … had you and…"

When I talked to him, he said he had no idea that you were 15 or 16 – he said that you told him you were 18.

"Na … that ain't true…that ain't true. He knows my age. I had a mom with a big mouth, straight up – she let him know. You know…. It is what it is. If you don't know she would tell somebody…. And that ain't something to tell a lie about. So…"

How does your mom relate to you?

"I was rebellious in my ways you know ... I was the type when I was 14; I always used to take care of myself. I had a father who had money, I was kind of spoiled in a way – I did what I wanted to do. You know ... and my dad gave me that cash, its not like I didn't have anything ... 16. I moved out of the house but she wanted to keep the kids. I let the kids stay with her but I left and always took care of myself."

How's your relationship been with Andre as I have grown up?

"Oh the pits ... the pits.... He was thinking he'd regret it, but I don't regret you! He was just.... He was so ... not my type of a guy. Mistakes do happen but you are the blessing that came out of it so.... I can't be too mad."

My dad said that you guys had talked about getting an abortion?

"Yea, he wanted to ... he wanted to. But I didn't do it because my mom didn't believe in it– I had to go with what she said."

He also talked about child support.

"Yea, he had to take care of his kid! He wasn't coming around once a month saying here's a hundred and fifty dollars, it could help with something. He wasn't that type of guy...." "You know...He's the type of guy you make something you forget about it" So how do you go about something like that? Wouldn't child support be the proper way? "Yea and I put him on child support and he never paid it"

I want to know why you hit me over the head with a glass plate?

"I did... Yea I did... Yes I did. I had stayed away, the way I felt, I had been gone and I come home and I had been telling you to do this do that ... and you had been on your own for a little while so you thought you didn't have to listen to me anymore so on...so on ... so on. It was something you said that was disrespectful and before you knew .... I hit you, not meaning to but it was my actions just because I don't care how long your mother stay away, just like your other brothers and sisters I tell them this, what your parents do…. How they do and stay away…. The bible tells you that you are to respect your mother and father regardless of…Every time you give it to the Lord the Lord would handle it, instead of taking it into your own hands. So at that one time I did feel that you were a little disrespectful to me so you know…. I did hit you with a glass plate – I can't take that back, its over with and all we can do is move on!"

But hitting your child with a plate?

"You were not a child, you were 18.
I wasn't 18, I was 16!"

"Yes you were—but you still got hit with a glass plate and I aint taking that back! Yea but like I said I cant go back, yes it was but I didn't kill you! Some mommas murder their kids but I just hit you with a plate – you don't disrespect me no more when I tell you to do something."

I didn't disrespect you I replied quickly. You don't remember You were just mad at something and took it out on me
"Whatever, Alcee!' she replied

I have been on my own for quite a while now. Tell me about that experience for you as a mother knowing that I was on the streets by myself.

"On the streets, what do you mean on the streets?"

Being on my own, having two jobs, having to get my own place as a high school kid – doing all of this did not get to you as a mother? Wasn't there something you wanted to do about that?

"No…Not in the slightest, instead it made me proud! I did the same thing much younger than you and I was a girl, I didn't accept anything from no one. I was 16; I wanted to get my own place, live my own life. I'm not looking out for anyone to be sorry, that's what I wanted and that's what I went for. I was looking at you as another me but as a boy. So I wanted to see you do those things! Its like life you learn that during your early years, its not like you had to do that. Half of the time I wouldn't even be home … hell …. You had the house – but its just what you wanted to do, you wanted to strive and I wouldn't come in the way – I would step back and let you. You know … if you fall I had been there. People do what they want. I don't have to worry about you committing no crimes because you're an honest working man. I respected that."

What do you think the future holds for you and I?

"You know, I think it's going to be ok. I'm going to go back and get more education for nursing and in five years you are going to be on track and I'll be on my track. I pray to God that those girls get on their track… Because those girls are a whole other breed so I think it's going to work itself out."

Tell me about your relationship with my sisters, "those girls"?

"Um … My girls do a lot of things that I don't approve of, it's a whole other generation and a whole other ball game and you know … I tell them what's right and what's wrong and I tell them what I expect from them and you know but…But I let them live their life because experience is the best teacher to me…So you know … I let them live. But like I said whenever they need me, whenever they need my advice the truth, I'm gonna give it to them and they could always pick up the phone and call me."

Do you or did you ever want to take care of your daughter after she was shot and live with knowing that she is now in a wheel chair running the streets?

"Yea… I wish I could touch her make her change her ways but…. I'm a nurse and I took care of her and when it happened I was like good because I already knew the skills to take care of her. But my daughter wanted to bring guns into the house, my daughter wanted to bring drugs into the house, my daughter had respect for nobody's house – so…. I had to do something. For a while she was here until I found a gun on the floor, now let me remind you that I have a 4 year old and I have my other son. On the floor and its loaded, so what is a mother to do? I took the gun; I took it and threw it away. She went balastic on me because of it. That's why she's in the wheelchair now because of stuff like that, why would you carry a gun? What are you still in this kind of life? She wouldn't abide by nobody's rules! She's welcome to come here anytime she wants but I'm not going to tolerate the guns, the drugs, and all sorts of her friends running in and out."

Why have you not come to visit me up at school?

"I just got off probation a year ago."

Probation? For what?

"I flew from the cops."

Why were they after you?

"Because the girl I was with picked something out of the store and brought it to my car." "So I was put on three years probation and I just successfully completed that so now I can come visit you."

Do you know how I'm doing at school or what I'm studying?

"You are studying like detective right?"

I would like to someday work for the FBI or be a schoolteacher

"Oh. Didn't know that, she replied," she replied in a surprised and sarcastic voice

It was in a manner like I proved her wrong

There was a serious void of parental support and character examples but there were other people who filled that void for me that you as a mother and Andre as a father couldn't. As a parent knowing that you existed and were there but not there – how does that feel for you?

"Ok, so its like I could have been there and we could have been in a dark, poor, poverty struck neighborhood. "No!, its what I had to do to make it happen so that you can have school, you can have lights, you can have food, you can have water – its like you're not trying to not be there but you gotta do what you gotta do. If you felt like a void it's a misunderstanding, you knew that I had to do what I had to do – I was a single parent."

What exactly is it that you "had to do"?

"Work, make money, you know.... Pay the bills and go to school. I went to school, should've gone a little earlier in my younger years but…"

Many things have tarnished our relationship….

"But you got to realize that the world don't owe you nothing. You're 18 and you know I love you because you're my child and I would lay my life down for any of my children. But you can't progress without letting things go because once you let it go you have a cleaner slate."

What are you prepared to do, to fix this tarnished relationship? What have you tried to do?

"Well, I had already had the nursing license. Now I let everything, just everything works itself out on its own. Like I said, I'm not going to run them down, my kids know deep down inside that I'm a good mom, its just how the circumstances were. If some days the sun didn't shine good, doesn't mean that she's a bad mom so … I know I support you in whatever you do. I'm not emotional and to me it is what it is and that's what my children can't deal with because I'm just a straight out person – on the line."

What are you prepared to offer for the future that would ensure a positive relationship between you and all of your kids?

"You know I'm just going to be a mom, I'm going to be your mom – you can't change that and neither can I so ... whatever it takes ... whatever it is – whatever that needs to be fixed will be fixed, whatever is broken will mend eventually, that's how I look at it but I also have other younger children that I have to take care of and I feel like I did the best I could, they might feel I owe them something but I'm just going to be a mom! That's all I got."

When is my birthday?

"January the 31st, the 30th"?"

My birthday is the 30th

"I thought you were born on the 31st"

My father and you both don't know when my birthday is! Come on, I said to myself feeling embarrassed.

I feel like there is still a perpetuating bitterness for me.

"I don't know. I don't care"

It's not that you didn't care but I felt like you were never there for me when I needed it.

"I had to do what I had to do."

Christmas, you weren't there?

"I was in Jail how would I?"

Why were you in jail for Christmas that was a big holiday for me as a child?
"Cocaine"

Why! When you know you were all I had growing up?

"Because I was a kid myself."

You were grown enough to have sense to know you had kids, I said with a serious look. She kept beating around the bush and didn't want to own up to her faults

"Whatever Alcee! Are we done yet?"

No. Matter a fact yes. We are. Thanks for your time!

Now speaking about both of my parents, I love both of them with all my heart and I just wish that they were there for me when I needed them. They don't know what they missed out on. I always wanted both of my parents in my life like other kids I knew. When I had sporting events, I would be jealous seeing my teammates being congratulated by their parents. Eventually I became accustomed to it and it didn't bother me anymore. I realize that holding a grudge is not really a good thing to do. I felt that not talking to my parents would not make me a good person? I just always told myself that they do not know what their son has accomplished and how I changed my life and where I am headed in life. I forgive both of them and still wish they were in my life for both the good and the bad.

Even now, I still don't know or understand why my mom never liked me and treated me the way she did. So from me to my mother, if you're reading this book I've been waiting for the opportunity to tell you this. We've never had a relationship with one another. I want you to know that I was really afraid of you when you would swear at me and talk to me in so many bad ways. I never wanted to see you again or speak to you. I always told you that I was going to be the one who would succeed, but you never believed me. I forgive you and hope that we can develop a relationship. Another thing I want you to know is that I always forgave you when you went to jail and I always tried to impress you, but it just never seemed to work.

"I don't think my mother was honest and will ever take full responsibility for what she did, but it's okay because I got out the questions that I had wanted answers to for a long time and that is a great feeling." –Alcee Walker speaking about his mother, Caurise Walker.

Chapter 3: Broken Family of 7

"I am a gangster. This is no act. It is in my blood. I have never had a boyfriend. I don't like boys. I like girls." said my oldest sister Barbara Walker

    As the second oldest of seven children, I played a huge role in my younger siblings' lives. My oldest sister, Barbara Walker, dropped out of high school in the ninth grade to run the streets and sells drugs after my mother went to jail for the first time. In a recent interview with Barbara, I asked her why she decided to drop out of school and get involved with the streets. She simply replied, "School is not for everyone. I wanted to get some extra money to help Mom out." She then proceeded to say that she would someday like to go back and get a proper education but it is hard now. "The streets will mess you up, they messed me up," she said disappointedly. She now says she continues to run the streets and sell drugs to survive.

    It was up to me to replace Barbara and to be a good role model for the rest of my younger siblings. Barbara had a big influence on my life growing up. Not having a father in my life, she always guided me and supported me to go in the right direction. She would always tell me not to think or worry about my father not being in my life. It was hard for me to understand because obviously I would have loved for him to be around. Barbara would always say, "He is just a coward and a loser. He would not do anything for you even if he was around." Barbara's dad would spoil her and give her anything she wanted. She would act like he was my dad too, which was really nice. When they would go out to get new shoes, she would take me along. She wanted

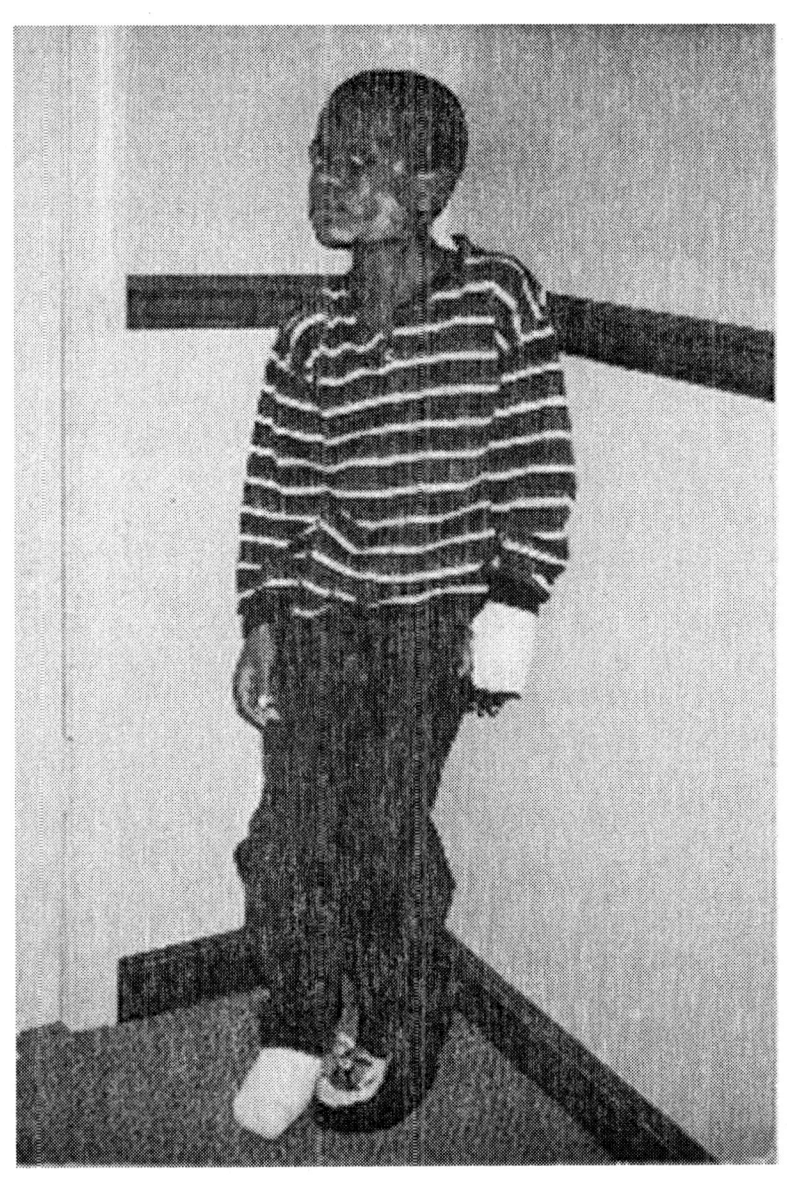

Childhood Burns

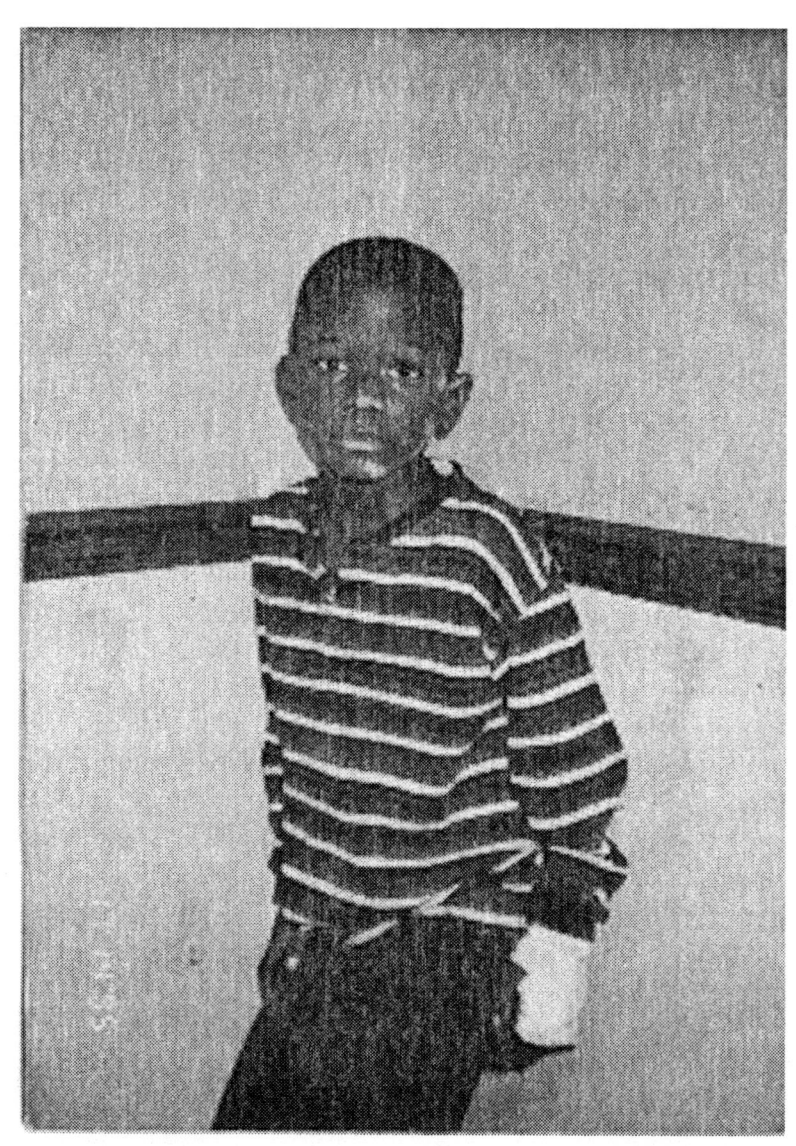

Childhood Burns

Childhood Burns

Dad

Dad

Mom

Mom

Mom

Barbara

Tameka

McKelton Family

Mr. Davis

me to feel like he was my father too, which I appreciated.

She was shot four years ago and is now paralyzed from her waist down and is in a wheelchair for the rest of her life. I hate to see her like this because she has a lot of potential and is very smart. During the interview, Barbara told me about the incident in more depth. "It was drug related. I got into an altercation with someone over a drug deal and I was just in the wrong place at the wrong time. I have been in a wheelchair for about four years now.

"You know I do remember the night you got shot." I had just gotten out of work and I was riding my bike home in the rain. My phone kept ringing and ringing in my pocket. I didn't want to take it out of my pocket because it was raining so hard. I got home and saw that there were eight missed calls from my cousin. I knew something was up. I called her back and she was yelling into the phone asking where I was. "Barbara just got shot!" she yelled to me. My heart started beating fast. I was so scared about whether or not she was going to make it. My cousin had said she was in the Intensive Care Unit in the hospital. The First thing that came to my head was that I hoped she didn't pass away, I was praying she would make it. I called a cab and got a ride to the hospital. When I got to the hospital, all my family members were outside crying. They wouldn't let me go see her at first. I finally got in there and she was hooked up to all these machines and tubes and I couldn't believe it. I was speechless. I really thought I was going to lose her that night. I would look at her and she could not open her eyes up all the way. I knew she recognized me, though. I just sat there, asking "Why? Why?" [Tears were rushing out of my eyes.] Even though we were always fighting at home, she was always there for me, more than anyone in my family. I couldn't lose her; she was all I had. It wasn't time for her to go yet. In the interview Barbara says how lucky she is to still be here because she could have easily been killed instead of paralyzed.

I also wanted to know about her relationship with my mother. I never really noticed how they got along because we were never really all in the house together. Barbara would always be running away and such. However, she said that the relationship has gotten better since they have both gotten older and more mature. "We didn't really get along when I was young because I was always running away from home. I felt like she was putting too much pressure on me about taking care of the little siblings and everything.

Now I am an adult and she is an adult and we talk to each other like adults. She respects me more now and so we don't have those issues we used to."

Barbara opened up about another aspect of her life during the recent interview. She explained she is a lesbian and she has only ever dated girls. "I am a gangster. This is no act. It is in my blood. I have never had a boyfriend. I don't like boys. I like girls." Barbara always dressed like a boy when we were younger. She was always a tomboy. I thought she would grow out of the stage but she just never did. It started becoming more and more clear that she really wanted to be a guy. Then when she got caught up in the streets, she came out. She is still the same person though. Her personality did not change so even though it doesn't always make sense to me, I accepted her for her decision.

To this day, Barbara will still call and ask how everything is and make sure I don't need anything. Now I feel like I am her big brother, though. Since I made better decisions through my life, I make sure she is all right. She is paralyzed in a wheelchair, so I am always worried about her. I disagree with a lot of her decisions but we will always support each other. My dream is for her to come up to St. Lawrence someday and watch me play in a football game before I graduate. She always supported my sports and I would love for her to be able to watch me play.

I have a younger sister, Caryan Walker who is 19 years old. When she was in elementary school, she did so well in school. She was a very smart girl and always received good grades. She was involved in school activities, as well. I was the one always getting into trouble in school. Even though I was older than her, I felt like she tried to keep me in line when we were younger.

However, the trouble started in middle school. She went from this nice, smart, young girl to getting into fights and getting in trouble in school and not caring about her education. She also began to date girls. She followed in Barbara's footsteps in some ways because she dropped out of school before reaching high school. She runs the streets and thinks that's a cool thing to do.

Caryan was the one I got along with the most out of all my sisters. She was the one that supported me and would help me with my schoolwork. To see her turn out the way she did was very disappointing. It is sad because she was on the right track in so many ways but she threw it all away. She was very smart and always made good grades. When she dropped out of school and wanted to run the streets I was mad but really couldn't really do anything about it. Over the years our relationship has gotten a lot stronger and I have talked to her about getting her life back together and going back to school. Going to into my second year of college I can recall her helping me pack all of my belonging to go back school and finds herself a little jealous sometimes because she really doesn't know how it feel to leave for college and wishes she had stayed in school. Now she is trying to get her GED and apply to community colleges. I feel like I had a big influence on her for why she is trying to turn her life around. I think seeing me go to college and succeed makes her want to do the same thing.

Caryan does not have a good relationship with our mother. Through out her life she considered her father a stranger and just recently found out that she and my oldest sister Barbara have the same dad. All these years she never really knew that they had the same father. She does not really talk to him either. She told me that she loves them because they are her parents, but that is the extent of it. They were never there for me growing up so I don't feel the need to have a relationship with them. She told me recently that she talks to them more now that she is older and more mature, but not a lot. Again, if our mother had guided her more when she was younger, she wouldn't have to try and pull her life together now. She would already be on the right track.

My next youngest sister is Ashley Williams, who is 17 years old. When she was younger, she would wear skirts, wear her hair nicely, and she made the honor roll several times in school. We would always talk and I would make sure she had some money for things she might need. The turning point for Ashley came when she was going into high school. She began to change her way. She turned her ponytails into dreadlocks. She began to steal cars, run from the police, and get involved in gangs. Along with my other two sisters, she began to date girls. As she got older, she became more and more involved in the streets.

Ashley's father died when she was about 7 years old. He was murdered in a drug-related situation and was thrown into a lake. She tells me now that she has a closer relationship with our mother. Now that they are both older, Ashley is trying to follow in her father footsteps and live up to his reputations.

Our relationship is the worst out of all my sisters. She refers to me as the "good boy," "white boy," or "school boy" because I decided to go to college. In her mind, that is not cool. I always ask her when she was going to get her life together and she always replied, "College is not for everyone. I like being a thug." I think she is jealous of the life that I am living now, but she would never admit that.

She now attends a "Drop back in" high school. This is a high school for students who are in danger of dropping out. She thinks that when I try to give her advice, it is to bring her down. She will never listen to me and always gets very defensive if I try to talk to her. Hopefully she will graduate high school and get her life on track someday. I don't think it will be anytime soon, unfortunately.

My baby sister is Janatuica Cabrera, who lives with her grandparents. She is now 13 years old. I also have seen her grow from a little baby to a nice young girl. She is in great hands with her grandparents because they are taking good care of her. They have full custody of her and are making sure she gets her education. She ended up with her grandparents because when she was in 1st grade, she stole $20.00 from our mother. My mother found out that she did this and gave her a beating. Janatuica was going to visit her grandparents for a weekend and told them what had happened. Her grandparents then decided to take it to the court and they received full custody of her. I can remember social workers coming to the house and asking me questions about what had happened.

When she was living with us at the house, I would walk to the bus stop to pick her up. She would come running off the bus towards me and tell me everything she did in school and all about her friends. It was almost like I was her father figure, and it good to influence her life so positively.

I had not seen Janatuica since she was in the 1st grade and now she is in the 6th grade. This past summer I was determined to see her before I came back to college no matter what I had to do. I searched for her grandparent's phone number and luckily I came across her father in the store. I called and told her I was coming to see her and she was excited to hear from me after not hearing from me in years. The day before I left for my second year of college I set up a date to go see her. I was so speechless to see her. She had grown in many ways and looked so different. Tears rolled from my eyes as if I was watching my own daughter grow up after all this time. I didn't know what to say to her for about 2 minutes. Going into middle school and playing softball, I couldn't be happier for her. Since she is in good hands with her grandparents, I don't feel like I need to worry about her. I think her grandparents saved her life by gaining custody of her.

I also have two little brothers, Juan Cabrera and Jayvon Walker. Juan is ten and the Jayvon is 4 years old. Juan was never really around our house. He always stayed with his godmother. I saw him when he was born, though. Since I lived with my mom for the most time out of all my siblings, I saw them all being born. I would see them for only a little while and then their grandparents or godparents would take them away from my mother. I was his big brother but I don't feel like I could build that "big brother" relationship with him because he was not living with us.

One Christmas, he had wanted a video game. I remember I was on my last $100.00 since I was living on my own. However, I really wanted to get it for him. I could remember all the Christmas holidays' when I did not get what I wanted and I realized I needed to get it for him. I wanted to be a good big brother because I always wanted a big brother growing up.

He runs through my mind a lot because I am his big brother and I want to be a part of his life. When I do see him, he always wants me to play wrestling with him because that's his favorite sport. He always asks me when I am going to buy him a wresting video game. I always laugh and tell him he doesn't need to be playing or watching that because he could get hurt and he always says "Man, I am not going to get hurt." I know the directions he's going in with his godmother are right directions because she makes sure he gets his schoolwork done and makes good grades.

Even though I am not around much because I am always up at school, I know that when I graduate and get a job, I can fulfill all those brotherly duties. I want to see him do well and get back to being a big part of his life.

Jayvon is the youngest out of all of us. He is very special in many different ways. He's very smart for his age and picks up concepts really fast. I was shocked that I was having another little brother and wanted to be a part of his life right away. Growing up in the house with him for about two years was the best part of my life. After those two years was up, we started to go our separate ways. When I left to live on my own, he was still living with our mother. When our mother went to jail, I would look out for him. I felt like more of a father figure than a brother. I didn't see him that much my 11th and 12th grade years of high school and I was depressed and worried about him a lot. When I moved out of the house, he would always ask why I left. I couldn't sit there and tell him it was because I didn't like our mother. I always had to sugarcoat it and tell a slightly different story. By not having a good relationship with my mother, it is affecting my relationship with Jayvon, which is very unfortunate.

Now, he always asks me where I have been and I tell him college, and he asks if he can come with me. Jayvon is the one I live for and will keep pushing for him so that he doesn't have to go through what I have been through, and can always have what I never had.

I never see any of my sisters or brothers on a regular basis and often worry about how they are doing. Most of all, I worry about my sisters Barbara, Caryan and Ashley. The three of them are still running the streets. I am worried about Barbara because she is still doing the same things she did before she was shot. I don't think she took it seriously enough when she was shot. I don't think she knows how much of an impact that event had on my life. She won't listen to anyone and does what she wants to do. I have seen a change in Caryan. I see that she is trying but she does not have the help and support that she needs. I always call and check up on her to make sure she has what she needs. To be honest, I don't see Ashley changing at all. There is only so much you can say until you just get tired of trying to get her to change. I am not going to give up though. I want to see her get her high school diploma. I know what it feels like to have people give up on you. I still love her and I want the best for her even though we don't get along well. I rarely talk to Janatuica. I know there is going to be one day when we re-connect our relationship. I know she is going to be fine, get through school, and be successful. Even though she was not dealt the right cards, she is driven. I miss her a lot but I can't really do much while I am up here at school. For my little brothers, I feel like I could have been a better brother, but I had a lot to deal with myself. I wish I had more time to spend with them and be that great big brother. I let the relationship with my mother interfere with the relationships with my little brothers. Overall, I love them all and always miss them. I wish our mother could have done something right and had us all in one house. I think if we had each other in the same house, we could talk to each other about all of our problems.

"I pray that Barbara, Ashley, and Caryan all get on the right track. As Ashley gets older, I am sure she will realize that she cannot do anything without an education. Eventually, I think we will see eye to eye. For my little brothers, once I am situated I will be a better big brother. For my youngest sister, I miss you." –Alcee Walker speaking about his sisters and brothers.

Chapter 4: High School Friends

Throughout my life, I have met many people with whom I developed good relationships. As I got older, I began to realize the value of good friends. Going into high school with the friends I grew up with, we had a pact to stick together no matter what happened. However, that changed once we entered high school.

My best friend was Lamar Dawkins; I first met Lamar in the 6th grade. He was a new student in our class. When he first came into class, everyone laughed at him because he was so big. He sat right in front of me and he did not come prepared to class at all. I'm talking no pencil, no paper, nothing. He turned around and asked me if I had anything to write with. I told him I did not have any extra supplies. He told me "Fuck you, then!" I thought it was pretty funny. From then on, we started hanging out all the time. Lamar was a pretty good basketball and football player. In the eighth grade, I had moved and had to transfer middle schools. I did not know it, but sure enough Lamar was transferring to the same middle school. We were so shocked to see each other again and we were able to hook back up. In 9th grade, he moved to my neighborhood so we became even closer. We went to the same high school and were inseparable. The turning point came going into 10th grade. He decided to change and that had a big impact on my life. He first started going downhill when he snatched a lady's purse on the street. He did not have a car or anything but he would use public transportation to get to a busy area of the city. If he saw a lady who was alone or an elderly lady, he would go up and talk to them. He would say something that made them look through their purse and then he would grab it and run. The first time he did this, he had asked me if I wanted to come with him. The police caught him that first time. He was put in a detention program for about 6 months. When I didn't hear from him that night, I thought something was up. I heard through other friends that he had gone to jail. I had really wanted to go with him because I needed fast money. However, something was telling me not to go and I went with that instinct. He dropped out of school in 10th grade. After he was finish with the program, his mentality was even worse. He didn't care about getting caught by the police or whose things he was stealing. He then became an even worse criminal. He began to break into people's homes and smoke marijuanna. He was in and out of jail from then on. Every time I saw him, I was so disappointed at what had gotten into him. He changed so fast right before my eyes. I have matured so much since I have been in college. I have realized how much I have going for myself. I can recall summer break after my freshman year. I was driving to get some gas for my car. The light was about to turn red and I saw this big kid in the middle of the road. I saw him crossing the street and I couldn't believe it was lamar. I yelled out to him and he said "Hey! Pull over, come over here!" I did a U-turn and pulled next to him. It was really good to see him. I told him how I had just finished my first year of college and he said he had been doing the same old stuff. I gave him a ride home and gave him my number so that we could meet up. However, I then realized I had way too much to lose by hanging out with him and getting into the lifestyle he lives. I ended up not calling him for this reason. I then saw him again over Christmas break. I was sitting on a park bench and he called my name. He got out of the car and he was so skinny. He had two black eyes. He looked so awful. He told me he had just gotten out of prison. He had tried to rob someone that was an undercover cop. He was in jail for about 5 months and had been beaten up by the men in there. He was getting a haircut at the same place I was, at my uncle's shop. My uncle told me "I know he is your friend, but you can't hang around with him anymore." That was the last time I heard from him or saw him.

I first met Jim Louis, another good friend, when we were eleven years old at a basketball camp. He didn't like me because I was scoring all my team's points. He wanted to fight me after the game. Four or five years later, we ended up in the same English class. I was a new student in his class. When I saw him and we made eye contact, the memory of him wanting to fight me seeped into my mind. The teacher put me next to him and we were friends from there on out. When I got kicked out of the house and he got into fights with his stepfather, we would just sit outside and talk for hours. He lived about two blocks from where I did. I feel like I was an inspiration to him because he would see me doing well and wanted to do the same thing. When I transferred high schools, it was a test for him if he could make it without me after being so close for three years. He wanted to transfer as well but he did not have the grades to get in. He had to stay at his high school. Going into 12th grade, Jim had a baby. He became more mature because of this. Jim ended up graduating from high school. Jim lives in his apartment with his baby and his baby's mother. He works full time to support his family. I am not angry with Jim because he did not go to college like me. I respect Jim because he is a responsible father and he is dealing well with the situation. Sometimes he wishes he went to college so that he could get a better job, but he never got caught up in the streets. He is doing what he has to do and taking care of his first priorities, which is his baby.

Then there was Roy Rosemond' who was a big brother to me even though I had to grow up a little faster then he did. Out of all my friends, Roy and I became the closest. When I first moved to my neighborhood, my neighborhood had a football team. They needed a quarterback so I tried out for the position. I made the team. Roy played runningback. He always wanted me to throw the ball to him. I didn't know how good of a football player he was and he didn't know how good of a player I was. One play, I decided to throw the ball to him. He scored a touchdown! I was so shocked and I had underestimated him. We went to high school together. The day I got kicked out of my house with all my clothes and everything, I moved in with him. I had six bags of clothes and he helped me drag all six bags into his room. He had two brothers, one sister, a mom, a stepdad with him, all living in the same house. I stayed with him for four or five months. His parents treated me like I was one of their sons. We went to school together, we did everything together. He was like my real brother. They didn't ask me for any money for rent or food or anything. One morning, his mom went to get the car to take us to school. I came down first and got in the car with her. She then told me I had to find somewhere else to stay. It was just getting too hectic in the house. She gave me a deadline to be out of the house. I was so sad. I didn't know where I was going to live or what I was going to do. I packed all my bags and had to be out by a certain date. I was crying while I was packing my bags. I didn't know where I was going to sleep. I was not angry with "Phat" or his mother. I thanked them for letting me stay there as long as they did without asking for anything. I would say it made my relationship with him even stronger. I always had to grow up faster than him because of the situation I was put into, but I was still his little brother. I then made the decision to transfer to another high school, which made it harder to stay in touch but we still did a little bit.

Another good friend was Travar Dixon. Travar and I became really good friends in the tenth grade. I always knew him but we never hung out. We lived in different towns, so we would only see each other in school until 10th grade. During 10th grade we did everything together. We played on the same junior varsity team basketball. He refused to pass the ball to me; he would always just shoot the ball himself. When we had an away basketball game, I didn't never have a ride home and neither did Travar. He would call Mr. Davis because he lived right down the street from him. One night, Mr. Davis came to get him and Travar asked if I could get a ride with him too. He said "No problem!" and he brought me home that night. Travar and I would always get into trouble together. I remember he got into fights and was suspended from school. We were in the same Spanish class. We had no idea what was going on in the class and we had an exam the next day. We decided to steal the answer key from the teacher's office. I went and got the answer key and he was the look out. We were running down the hall, so happy we were going to pass the test. Little did we know, it was the wrong answer key! One day at a girl's basketball game, I had a conversation with a football coach from another high school. He was asking if I wanted to transfer and play for his team. This all sounded so good but I didn't want to leave the school where I was popular, where my friends were, and where my girlfriend was. I didn't want to go alone so I asked Travar to transfer with me. I wanted him to come and play basketball for the school. He was so excited about it and we both ended up transferring to that high school. We were so worried that we wouldn't have friends at the new school, but it was the best decision we have ever made. That is what got us to where we are today. I would pick him up every morning for school. We started to really focus, do our work and go to class; things we never did at our old school. We graduated together, which was an amazing feeling. Everyone had doubted us, but we made it. He enrolled in Florida Memorial University with a business major.

Last but not least, I met a family in Boynton Beach, Florida Marvin and Mara Blitz, who not only contributed to my life in high school, but also followed me to college. I was the high school player of the week for football and had an opportunity to have an article written on me about my life. When the '*Survival of the Fittest*' article was printed in the Ft. Lauderdale *Sun Sentinel* newspaper in the fall of 2006, Mr. Blitz just happened to be reading this article and then shared it with his wife, Mara. They then contacted me by mail and gave me a check for two hundred dollars. Later they helped me get my vehicle repaired. This family and I became good friends and they have supported me in many ways, such as attending my graduation and scholarship ceremonies. They have also given me advice on college and have sent me many care packages. Marvin and Mara have made a big difference in my life; by making sure I grow and mature. They give me life advice that I will always be able to use. I know that they will be reading this book and I would like to tell them thanks for everything and I really appreciate their help and guidance. This family has helped me grow from a little boy to a young man. Recently, they got on my case about needing better manners and etiquette. They also thought I needed to learn how to write better thank you notes. Even though I was mad at the time, I know they just want the best for me and want me to succeed to my full potential.

All my friends impacted me in their own way. In school, other students would call all of us thieves. We weren't necessarily thieves, we just had a desire to get money and we couldn't find a job other than coming up with this next plan to get some extra money.

It was an everyday hustle to have money. We would stand on the "meter," or that median that divides the lanes of the street. We would put on our team jersey and make these money buckets that had signs that would say we were trying to raise money for our basketball team to go on a tournament. We would make a sign saying, "Please help our basketball team go to a tournament in Atlanta, thank you!" We would go every Friday and Saturday when we knew it was payday and make from at least $70 to $90 a day. Everyone would get his own section of the meter. You got to keep whatever was in your bucket. We went so often because we knew it was fast money. People started to realize that we were overdoing it. We got a warning from the sheriff saying that if he saw us back out there we would go to jail. That still didn't stop us. One Friday afternoon, we were out there and six or seven officers rushed up to us. We all just took off running full speed. We ended up getting away by jumping in a cab. The cab driver didn't want to take us because there were so many of us. We then showed him all our money so he let us in. We got to the grocery store and changed our change into dollars and it was all ours.

Even though I had to grow up faster than all my friends, we always stuck together. None of us had a father in our lives. We made plenty of mistakes and did things we should not have done, but they were like my three brothers. They made growing up so much easier. Even though I was always the one that needed a place to stay, they still accepted me for who I was and always helped me out when I needed it. I love them all. Even though we didn't have fathers to teach us how to grow up as men, we taught each other how to be men. We made a promise to each other that whoever made it out first and whoever gets a successful job first, is going to come back and bring the rest of them up to succeed.

"I love Lamar like a brother and I hate not being able to be around him because we were so close, but I have too much to lose. I guess I just have to move on with my life. I really respect Jim because he is taking care of his priorities and being a man by taking care of his family as a young teen. Roy, I will never forget how you helped me drag my bags all the way to your house, I appreciate it. Travar we are almost there man, let's keep moving. Mr. and Mrs. Blitz, thank you for all your advice and support. Thanks to you, I know how to write a proper "thank you" note!" – Alcee Walker speaking about his friends.

Chapter 5: A Special Young Lady With a Magnificent Family!

"Alcee was out of control when I first met him. He was trying to impress me with things that I was not impressed by. I had to put him in check by telling him if he wanted to date me he had to get in gear because I don't date dummies" Tameka Speaking about her relationship with Alcee Walker

"I got to know Alcee as a chauffeur for Tameka, I would take her everywhere to see him. Now I feel like he is my son even though I didn't have him" Patreka Mckelton speaking on her relationship about Alcee Walker.

"He was brave enough to come to our house and ask my husband if he could date our daughter. I told him, I am not giving you permission to do anything else with my daughter you can keep her company and that's it" Miranda McKelton speaking on her daughter relationship with Alcee Walker.

It was the beginning of my tenth grade year at Palm Beach Lakes High School. I kept passing this one gorgeous young lady in the hall way over and over again. I did not think I would ever be able to date her because she was so attractive. I didn't think she would ever want to date someone crazy like me. After about two weeks of seeing her, I decided to approach her. Her name was Tameka and she was in the ninth grade. My boys and me usually didn't date girls younger than us because our motto was to aim for the older girls. There was something about Tameka that drew me to her. I asked her if I could have her phone number. She quickly responded, "No." At this point, my heart dropped and I felt rejected. I dropped my head and then she said, "But I can have yours." I felt relieved to hear that and I just smiled. That's how it all started.

Tameka called me a few days later and we started talking more and more, getting to know each other. I was hesitant to open up and tell her about my family situation because I didn't know what she would think of me after that. However, when I did open up to her, she did the opposite of what I had expected. She was very supportive about everything.

Tameka took school very serious and did extremely well in all her classes. Unlike me, I was still getting bad grades, getting suspended from school, not going to class, and hanging out with my friends. When I first met her she said I was out of control. I was trying to impress her with the materialistic things such as money, jewelry, and clothes. These were things that she was not impressed by. She said if I wanted to date her I had to get my act together because she doesn't date dummies. I thought to myself, was I a dummy or the things I partook in. She did not like what I was doing with my life. I knew I had to change at that point because I really wanted to date her. She expected more from me and she knew I had a lot of potential. My D's soon turned to A's and B's and before I knew it, I was on the "most improved student's list." She gave me the confidence to improve my grades and be the best student I could be. Because Tameka cared so much, it gave me hope. I knew that if I put my mind to it, I could do better.

Tameka was an amazing basketball player, which made me even more attracted to her. She was well known in school and her games were always packed because people wanted to see her play. She was always in the newspaper and being interviewed by reporters.

We would hang out in school and I would offer to buy her lunch, but once again she said, "No, I got my own money."

We had been talking in school for about seven or eight months before I went home with her to meet her family. She said I would have to ask her parents for permission in order to date her. I remember driving over to her house and when we reached the front door I began pacing back and forth. I was hesitant to enter Tameka's house. So many things crossed my mind. I didn't know what to say or if they would like me. I was hoping and praying that they didn't ask about my grades. I sat down with her parents and they gave me a run down of what they expected from me if I wanted to date their daughter. The most memorable moment was when her mother said "I am not giving you permission to do anything else with my daughter than to keep her company and that's it. " I really didn't know what to say so I just smiled and said yes ma'am. As I began to hang around their house more; they all began to learn about my family situation. I especially began to bond with Tameka's older sister, Patreka. Who in a recent interview said, "I got to know Alcee as a chauffeur for Tameka, I would take her everywhere to see him. Now I feel like he is my son even though I didn't have him. " We became so close that she felt like she was my biological mother. She even paid for my airfare to a basketball camp one summer! She supported me through everything. Patreka had a huge impact on my life. She always believed in me and really played a motherly role in my life. The Mckelton family was not wealthy by any means. They were just filled with a lot of love and kindness. It was not like they had extra money to support me, they truly wanted to help me because they all had very big hearts.

During the holidays, if I did not have anywhere to go, I would spend it with the McKelton family. Her father took me to get my first vehicle and get the car registration and everything. The McKelton family was a family that I could count on. They truly made me feel a part of their family. There were more of them at my high school graduation than there were members of my family.

Tameka also had a younger brother and an older brother. They accepted me for who I was, as well. I was very close with them too. Every member of the family was supportive and I loved spending time with all of them.

When I transferred to Inlet Grove High School, we had an orientation day that a parent needed to attend. Miranda, Tameka's mother, came with me and pretended she was my mother. From the time I met her, she supported me emotionally; they all did.

In the beginning, I had to ask if I could go to their house. Now, I stop by whenever and it feels like home. This family has been by my side from day one and I am very blessed to have them in my life. Tameka, without you and your family I have no idea where I would be at this point. Your family has been there for me every step of the way and words cannot express on how I would like to thank your family. Patreka, I don't know where to begin. I just want to say I love you and thank you so much for picking me every morning for school even when I had you waiting because I was never ready and I would just be getting out the shower. Thank you for making sure I didn't have to walk to school and making sure that I had enough money on my trip to Messiah Basketball Camp. The McKelton family is known as the perfect family in my heart.

"When I was in the tenth grade I though her family hated me because I never really came around. At her basketball games I was never sure if I should sit with them so I always sat with my friends. But now I am a McKelton and I am apart of there family and it's a blessing" Alcee Walker speaking on his relationship with the McKelton family.

Chapter 5: Those Old High School Days

"Now that I am older, I regret goofing around in high school because I feel at a disadvantage in college because I came here having learned nothing from high school. It is disappointing feeling like you are not as prepared for college as most of the students at St. Lawrence." –Alcee Walker speaking about his education.

I went to high school at Palm Beach Lakes High School, located in West Palm Beach, Florida. Going into the 9th grade, my behavior was a big problem. My schoolwork nearly had me in the last percentage in my class. I was put into a special program in school because my behavior was so bad. The program was for students that stayed in one classroom all day to do their work. These students had more disabilities than I did. Being in this program made you the victim of kids making fun of you. If you got caught coming out of that building, you would be mocked. I didn't want to do any work. I was stubborn. I only cared about impressing girls and showing off my money that I made from working. I only cared about fashion. I wanted to be popular and wanted everyone to know me. I wanted to get out of that building so that I could be popular. Sometimes I would skip school or leave early. I was always showing up to class late. If I got called on in class and I didn't know the answer, I would just say something like, "I don't know, ask someone else." I was not good at reading. I found out what I had to do to get out of this building. I was not on track to pass 9th grade, but when I found out what I had to do, I quickly changed and was able to as well to get out of the special building.

When I made it to the 10th grade, I had to take the FCAT, a standardized test in Florida. I failed the FCAT my tenth grade year. Without passing this test, you cannot get your high school diploma. I failed it in the 11th grade as well. I finally passed the reading section in the 12th grade but still had not passed the math section. Since I had been in that special program my freshman year, they waived the math section for me. That is why I could graduate high school.

The students at my high school only cared about fashion and how much money you had. No one cared about getting an education. It was all about who was popular, who was dating a hot girl, and who had a car. There was fighting and young girls were always getting pregnant.

The turning point for me came when one day I realized that I wanted to go to college, get a good job, eventually have a family, and get married. I knew I had to change my life around. What is after high school? I didn't want to work at Taco Bell my whole life. I wanted to go to college but I didn't have any money to go to college. I was not playing sports for a team, but I knew that was my only way to college. I decided I was going to try and get a football scholarship. The high school I was at seemed to only play their favorites. I thought that I should go to a school where the football team was not as strong so that I would stand out for recruiters. After talking to that coach at a basketball game, I decided to transfer to Inlet Grove High School. It was about 5 miles away from my current high school. It was a much smaller high school. The students were there to learn. They did not care about their fashion or money. Everyone was very disciplined. Everyone's goal was to get to college. I had to make some adjustments since it was much smaller. I knew I came for one reason, which was to try and get a football scholarship. I dominated football. I didn't tell him about my family situation because I did not know him very well. He was going to kick me off the team because my behavior was not appropriate. During a tournament my senior year, I wanted the ball every time to show my talent. I was frustrated that I wasn't getting it every time so I walked off the field and went home. [Then the article about me came out in the paper.] My coach had said he was not aware of all that went on in my life. After he found out, we had a much stronger relationship. I apologized and he let me have my spot back on the team. I would go to practice twice a week and I would work the other days. I was ranked second on the team. Since I only played my senior year, it set me back because no colleges had seen me play football. I then went to a football fair, where there were about thirty different colleges. I happened to run into the coach from St. Lawrence University. None of the division I ('D1') coaches really knew of me. I sent my highlights tape to many D1 programs, but got rejected from all of them. I knew any college was better than no college. I wanted to get as far as I could from where I was living now. After getting rejected from about 25 schools, I finally got accepted to St. Lawrence University. I told myself even if I did not like it, I would make myself like it because at least I was at college. Looking back at some of the guys I played sports with, some of them are not even in college. My plan was to do anything in my power to get as far from my situation as I could. St. Lawrence may not be the best situation but it's not the worst situation either. I am just very thankful and blessed that I have the opportunity to get a liberal arts degree.

Chapter 6: Just Couldn't Keep a Job!

"I needed money desperately, so I did anything in my power to get a hold of it no matter what I had to do now that I am older I am embarrassed" Alcee Walker speaking on his experiences with jobs.

My first job was working at Taco Bell. I was so excited about working and being able to provide for myself that I couldn't sleep the night before my first day of work. I rode my bike back and forth to work with my purple shirt, nametag, work boots, and hat to the side. My bike was an 18 speed, red and black mountain bike, which was my only means of transportation. I can remember getting picked on by my peers in high school who would drive by on my way to work. They would come to my job and pick on me while I was doing my job but I didn't care. I smiled and went back to work.

When I arrived to work the first thing I had to do was clock in and this was a great feeling to know that I was earning my own paycheck. It was a great feeling taking my card and swiping it in. I did not waste a minute because this was for my survival. I wanted all the hours I could get so that I was no longer dependent on my mother or father.

After the first week, I had worked a total of thirty hours. When I got my first paycheck, I didn't know how to read a paycheck. It was difficult to read because the hours and the money did not match up. I knew something was wrong because my first paycheck was only $25.00. I didn't want to ask my manager because I assumed I was reading it wrong and I didn't want to make him angry and get fired because I had just gotten this job.

After a few weeks of this going on, I finally got the guts to ask him about the situation. He just said to me that it would go on my next check. Not knowing what to do, I simply forgot about it.

I then began to build relationships with adults that worked there, as well. I would tell them about the situation and they told me he was known for stealing people's hours. They told me to ask for a receipt for my hours that I worked. That is what I started to do and it was then that I realized my manager really was stealing time from me. I had about sixty hours that were stolen from me. I worked my butt off for this company and on Sundays I would work double shifts so that I could provide for myself. I would come in from 8am to 4pm and then come back at 6pm and work until 10pm. I made sure I would have enough hours to make enough money so that I didn't have to ask anyone for money. I would not do my homework and fall behind in school to get more hours. I was so addicted to work and driven to always having enough money. I never wanted to have to depend on anyone. It was crucial I got the right amount because this was my one shot to take care of getting meals and clothes and anything I may need.

The last few weeks before school started that year, I worked a total of 96 hours so that I would have enough for school supplies and some new clothes. I kept every receipt in case my manager tried anything this time.

Making about $6.25 an hour, I was able to purchase all of my school supplies and uniforms for the upcoming year. After working for this company about a year and three months, things started to change. [The manager did not like the fact that I was starting to read the checks correctly and getting receipts so I finally realized what he was up to.]

Getting into altercations with the General Manager over my hours forced me to do something I really didn't want to do. Now looking back on it, I ask myself why I ever thought it was okay to do this. I was young and didn't know any other way to handle the situation.

Since the manager would not give me the correct paycheck', I would take money out of the cash register when I would be working on the front end. I would call my friend Jim Louis and have him come to my work and order a taco. He would pay for the taco but I would give him much more change than he should have gotten back. As soon as he walked in, we would make eye contact and I knew exactly what we were planning to do. Every time he came in, my heart would be pounding because I did not know what kind of trouble I would get in if I ever got caught. He would give me a 5-dollar bill and I would give him two 20-dollar bills back. He would walk off and after work we would divide the money up. This went on for about four or five weeks. I would not do it consistently every time I worked but randomly so that there was less of a chance of getting caught. I never was caught doing that.

Everyday after school I would have to go home and change into my work clothes. However, since I didn't have a key to the house, I had to wait for my mom to get home and let me in. Some days she would take hours to get home and let me into the house. I was constantly late for work and my manager began to get fed up with it. One day, he finally said something to me about being late. He started flipping out on me but I fought back because I was so angry with him for taking my hours and now yelling at me for being late. He told me I was fired from the job. I got so mad, I was swearing at him and I ripped my uniform off and threw it at him. I knocked over all the cups on the counter and stormed out the door. I was walking home so upset about what had just happened. Tears were streaming down my face as I slowly walked home. I had no idea what I was going to do now. I loved having a job and providing for myself: I had to. I could not believe I had just gotten fired from my job.

That didn't stop me though. About two months later, after living off of unemployment, I just moved on no more than two miles around the corner to work at Sam's Club. This company was much more organized than Taco Bell. I didn't have to worry about my hours being stolen. Starting out as a cart attendant making about $7.75 an hour, I was promoted into the warehouse as a sales associate in the electronics department. I wanted to earn more money so I tried to pick up as many skills as I could. I learned to run the cash register and drive a forklift during that first year.

I loved working and I had so many friends there with me. I was never supposed to get tips but I always would help people load their stuff in their cars and I would take the tips they gave me. Sometimes I would earn 30 or 35 dollars just in tips! I was never late for this job. I still had to walk to work but I didn't want to make any of the same mistakes that I had in my last job. I was very popular with the manager this time and other people I worked with. The managers always wanted me working in their departments.

Going into my second year is when all the trouble started. I began to feel so comfortable in the job and took it for granted. I would clock in and then leave for a few hours. I would also tell the personnel director that my hours were not showing up on my paycheck. For example, I would not work on a Sunday but tell them I did and they would give me that money in my next paycheck. I would just wander around and I stopped doing my job well.

My friend and I decided to try and pull something that was going to get us more hours than we worked. I told the company I had lost my time card, so they printed out a new one and I gave it to my friend. When my friend went into work, he would clock me in and I would not be there. One Sunday, my manager had seen that I was clocked in and he decided he wanted to come talk with me. He could not find me anywhere though. He called me over the loud speaker and I was nowhere to be found. My manager ended up watching the video of where we swipe our cards in and out. He saw what my friend had been doing, called him into the office and fired him right on the spot, not even giving him a chance to explain. The next day, when I came into work, the manager called me into his office. He said I could either tell the truth about what was going on or lie about it and get fired. I did not want to go behind my friend's back and tell the truth so I told the manager that I had no idea what was going on. He told me I was fired and to get out of his store. I knew it was my entire fault this time but I was still really upset. I was close with the manager and I really wanted to keep that job. I went to get something to eat at Taco Bell and just sat at the booth for about an hour. I could not believe what I had done and the opportunity I had just lost over money. Money was so important to me because I had no one to depend on for it and I did anything I could to get more of it. I felt awful about what I did and now had to move on to another job. I thought maybe I should just forget the job and sell drugs on the street. I knew what fast money that was and it was tempting at the time. However, I did not want to sink that low. I knew once I got involved in that, it was so hard to get out again.

After not finding another job, I was so frustrated. I decided to call my boy, "Big Money Mike." He was a huge kid and was very serious about his drug deals. I once saw him hit a kid across the face with his gun because he didn't give him the money that he owed him. He was a well-known drug dealer around my neighborhood. If you wanted to sell drugs, everyone knew to go to him. We were always close with each other. When I worked at Taco Bell, he would come in and I would give him free food. Even though he sold drugs, he knew I had more going for me. He knew I was always in school and playing sports. He asked me if I really wanted to get into the mess of the streets. I told him to "deal me in," which means that I wanted to start selling drugs with him. He did not give me the cocaine right away, though. He told me to take a couple days and think about it before getting myself into that. He knew I could have gotten addicted to it by seeing all that fast money. Luckily, I found a job before getting into it.

    I was hired at the check-cashing store. Little did I know this job would be where I made a mistake that would stick with me for the rest of my life. I was living in my own apartment. I was broke and focused only on one thing, which was getting money. I did not have enough money to pay my bills, put gas in my car, or even enough to eat. I had been working for about two weeks and I had figured out all the skills necessary to work there. I was so broke I decided I needed to come up with a plan. I was desperate. I worked around nearly twenty thousand dollars a day. I came up with a plan to get money quick. I figured out a scheme that would allow my friend who I knew and trusted to come into the store and make a western union transaction that they wouldn't pay and leave with a large amount of the company's money for free. The other employees were on a lunch break. I went to the front desk and did a western union transaction sent to my friend from a guy whose name I randomly made up. As I was printing the transaction, an employee came out of the break room. I ripped it out of the printer and pretended to throw it in the trash. The lady gave me a weird look but then thought nothing of it. I then called up my friend and said that my uncle sent me some money. I made up an excuse of why he didn't put it in my name and said he needed another one of my friend's name. My friend said, "Okay, we can get it after work!" I had not really thrown away the paper. It was balled up in my pocket. When I got off of work, my friend came and got me. We went to Publix to cash the check. I didn't want to get out of the car because I didn't want the cameras to see that I was with my friend. So, she went in and cashed it and handed me over five hundred dollars. I was saying to myself, "Wow, this really worked! I should do this more often!" I went to buy food, gas, and paid my bill. I was so happy. I got a phone call the next day from the lady that was training me at my job. She asked me if I misprinted a western union because the register was coming up five hundred dollars short. I denied it and said I didn't even know how to do that type of transaction. When I hung up with her, I started panicking. I couldn't believe I had screwed up again.

I was excited about going to work. I packed a lunch and was happy that I had some money in my pocket. The next day I reported to work and everyone immediately gave me this suspicious look. The managers were all there and they were all waiting for me. I heard the head manger on his cell phone. I heard him saying to the police, "Where are you? He is here!" They had got in touch with Publix, the grocery store where the check was cashed. This was right by my house, so I was first on their list of suspects. When I had heard him on the phone, I grabbed my lunch box and ran out the door. I left the store and went to my friend's house hoping that they wouldn't find me. I was trying to find the fastest way to get there without getting into an accident. I was so paranoid that they would come and arrest me when I was at my house so I didn't want to be there. I thought I would go to jail for sure.

They called and called and I didn't pick up the phone because I didn't know how to respond. They kept leaving me voicemails. They wanted me to come back to the store and I didn't want to because I was afraid of going to jail. This man then left me a voicemail saying that I was messing with much bigger law enforcement with this crime. He said they would press charges if I didn't come in. The company and I came up with an agreement for me to just pay the money back and I would be free so they ended up taking my check and leaving me with 65 cents.

I have dodged jail so many times with these jobs. They are all life lessons for me. I am so lucky that I still have never been arrested after these experiences. To be honest, going through these jobs and making those mistakes, it was terrifying. If I could do it over again, I would not have done any of those things and just done the jobs the way I was supposed to. Thinking about it now, it is hard to find a job and I took mine for granted. If I had never done what I did at Sam's Club, I would have probably still had that job today.

"I needed money desperately, so I did anything in my power to get a hold of it no matter what I had to do now that I am older I am embarrassed" Alcee Walker speaking on his experiences with jobs.

Chapter 7: A Mentor? Not a Father!

"While I am not his biological father, we developed a closeness and love for one another that translated from a mentoring relationship to a parenting relationship." – Ron Davis speaking about his relationship with Alcee Walker

I first met my mentor, Ronald Davis who I affectionately call '*Pops*', when I was in the tenth grade at Palm Beach Lakes High School. He was a mentor for my best friend, Travar Dixon. Pops would pick up Travar after our basketball games when he didn't have a ride home. I would be sitting around scrolling through my phone to see who I could call to come pick me up. Pops began to drive me home as well. That is how our relationship first started and began to grow. The first few times I hung around with Travar and Pops, I was just observing him. As we started spending more and more time together, I began to trust him. He could see my situation right through me; I didn't even have to explain myself.

Pops saw me as a young man with a lot of potential, but with no guidance or nurturing. He always guided me in the right direction. He knew he had to gain my trust before I was going to open up to him. He was honest and open with me. It took a long time, [but I eventually gained his trust.] He always said he had to "meet us where we were and bring us to where we wanted to go." This meant that Travar and I had been through many experiences that a teenager should not have had to go through so you could not impose on us. Pops knew we had to accept his help before making any progress. I was very independent because I had to grow up on my own and teach myself everything I knew. I wanted to do things my way. Pops was so patient with me and just kept supporting me no matter how many times I blew off his advice. I saw him almost everyday whether it was going out to eat or going to church or just hanging out talking.

I remember one time that I had absolutely no money and no gas to get back and forth to school. I didn't want to ask him for money but I just told him my situation. He told me at that moment that I didn't have to be afraid to ask for anything. He brought me right over to the gas station and filled my car up for me. After this situation, I finally felt like I had someone on my side. It was such a good feeling to know that someone was there if I needed something, someone to talk to me, and someone just guiding me in the right direction. It was not about him giving me money all the time; it was about his support and advice through "fatherly" eyes.

As my senior year started to wind down, I began to worry about whether I was ready for college or whether I was smart enough to go to college? Would I survive in college? Would I graduate from college. I had all these questions running through my mind but I had no answers. I would leave school around noon and I would drive for about seven or eight miles to Pops' office. I would just sit there until almost 5pm everyday! He would always ask me, "Any plans for college or anything?" I would simply reply, "I don't know, probably not."

He had my highlight tape for football and ordered about one hundred copies. He would send the tapes out everyday. He would have them sent as quickly as possible to the schools on our list. He would follow the tape up with a phone call to the head coach. He told me I would get into college, so not to worry! These are all things that my father should have done, but since I did not have his support, Pops would do this on his own time during his full time job.

I also developed a relationship with Pops' family. When I found out what college I was going to and it was time to prepare all my belongings, they all helped me out. His sister, who I call *Mama Pat*, bought me two large trunks to store my things in and bought me, sheets for my bed. Mama Pat made sure I had everything I needed before I left for school. They helped me ship everything to St. Lawrence and always provided care packages for me. Knowing that I have people on my side that can help me, I feel like I can achieve more. When I see that I have support from other people who really believe in me, it makes me work harder.

Another impact Pops had on me was that he got us into going to church and getting there on time. Travar and I would always come in late and Pops changed that. He would always tell us to build a relationship with God and we can't do that by hanging on the streets late at night. By hanging around Pops, I learned how to become a better young man. I learned how to respect people and how to be organized and on time for things. I started out as a kid, who did whatever I wanted to do. After hanging around Pops, I grew into someone who behaved well and gained maturity.

If it were not for you Pops, I don't know where I would be today. I really appreciate all that you have done for me including helping with the college process and giving me everyday life advice. I see a big difference in my life ever since I met you. You and your family are absolutely amazing. I feel like I am a part of your family because you treat me so well. I am not writing this book for people to feel sorry for me. I am not writing this book to get money. I just feel that if there were more mentors like you, Mr. Davis, I think that our society would be a lot different. Imagine how many kids are in my situation. I was going down the completely wrong path until I met Mr. Davis, who completely turned me around. You have helped me out in so many ways and the experience with you has been so good that it makes me want to help the next "Alcee Walker." Even though I never really listened to what you told me and still did things my way, it was great because I knew I could still call you after I screwed up and you would never gave up on me.

"While I am not his biological father, we developed a closeness and love for one another that translated from a mentoring relationship to a parenting relationship." – Ron Davis speaking about his relationship with Alcee Walker.

A Letter from Alcee H. Walker

Dear Readers,

As you can see, I had many obstacles to overcome throughout my life. Between parents, friends, and jobs, nothing came easy. When I decided to change my life around, I stayed disciplined, focused, and set goals for myself. As I look back on my teenage years and childhood years, I never imagined being where I am today let alone having a book published. If I had stayed on the track that I began on, I would be in jail, selling drugs, or even dead. I don't take complete credit for where I am today, because there are so many people, who made a contribution to my life and helped me get where I am today.

The purpose is to inspire kids who are in m position or a similar situation. I think society would become a lot better if we had more young people like myself to have an impact on people's lives. To those out there in my position, even if your cards were not dealt in your favor, you still have a shot. Everyone has a shot at making something of his or her life. You need to believe in yourself and find people who believe in you, as well. You have to surround yourself with positive people and stay focused on achieving one goal at a time.

Another piece of advice is to make the most of your education. Most of my school years, I would fool around, which only hurt myself and kept me from learning anything. Now, it comes back to haunt me during college because I do not feel as prepared as most kids. Education is your ticket out of whatever situation you may be in. You have to remember that and take it seriously.

The decision to attend a private, liberal arts university was probably the best decision of my life. Even though there were many adjustments to be made, I am thankful for where I am. It was hard coming from a predominately black neighborhood to a predominantly white environment. I am not used to being the minority, like I am here at St. Lawrence. I may not be in the best situation I would like to be in terms of being around my culture, but I am sure not in the worst and I am grateful for that. There have been many times where I just wanted to go back home, but then I think that there is nothing there for me to go back to. It is going to be the same as when I left. There are so many people who have faith in me and believe in me, even when I let them down. I am the first member of my family to graduate from high school and attend college. It is a good feeling, but I am not satisfied until I graduate from college, have a job, and have a wife and family. I want to be that father for my kids that I always wanted in my life. I want the opportunity to change the lives of young teens, like my life was changed.

We all know life is hard and we all have our own personal problems. It is about how you deal with those problems that builds your character. For me, Alcee Howard Walker, my journey has still not come to an end. If I had to live my life all over again, I would love to because it made me the man I am today. Remember, have goals, stay focused, and the main goal is to stay disciplined.

Sincerely,

Alcee H. Walker